For Maisie and Mason,
my first great niece and nephew

Alexandra Milton

First published in North America in 2022 by Boxer Books Limited.
www.boxerbooks.com
Boxer® is a registered trademark of Boxer Books Limited.

The illustrations were prepared using handmade paper,
torn and shredded with touches of color pencil.
The text is set in Bodoni 72 Old Style.
ISBN 978-1-912757-94-7

3 5 7 9 10 8 6 4 2

Printed in China
All of our papers are sourced from managed forests and renewable resources.

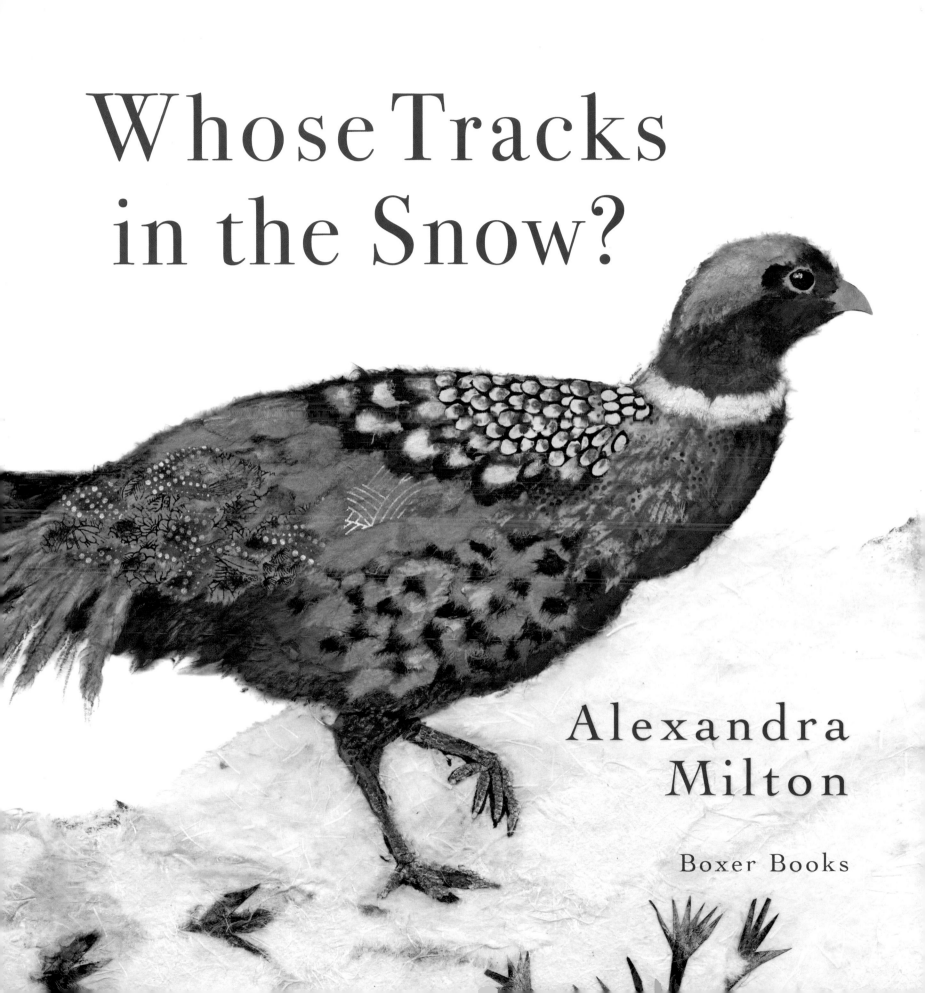

Whose Tracks
in the Snow?

Alexandra
Milton

Boxer Books

Look! Look!
Tracks in the snow!
Tracks that are oval,
Tracks that are round.

Who left the tracks
on the snow-covered ground?

A fast-running hare!

Hares are hoppers – their two smaller front paws touch the ground before their two larger hind feet. Unlike rabbits, they live above ground and run incredibly fast because speed is the best way of escaping danger.

Look! Look!
Tracks in the snow!
Tracks like hearts,
Tracks in two lines.

Who left
the tracks by the
snow-covered
pines?

A shy red deer!

Animals with hooves leave two long prints with a gap in between them: the pointy end shows the direction of travel.

Deer prepare for cold weather by eating lots of food and growing a winter coat with long thick hair. They hide under pine trees and move as little as possible to save their energy until spring.

Look! Look!
Tracks in the snow!
Tracks with three points,
Tracks like a wedge.

Who left the tracks by the snow-topped hedge?

A long-tailed pheasant!

Pheasants rarely fly and spend most of their life on the ground. They walk just like us, placing one foot in front of the other. In the day they hide in hedgerows, but at night they sleep in the low branches of a tree where they are safe. Often, many birds gather in the same tree with one keeping watch.

Look! Look!
Tracks in the snow!
Tracks like fingers,
Tracks with claws.

Who left the tracks in
funny groups of fours?

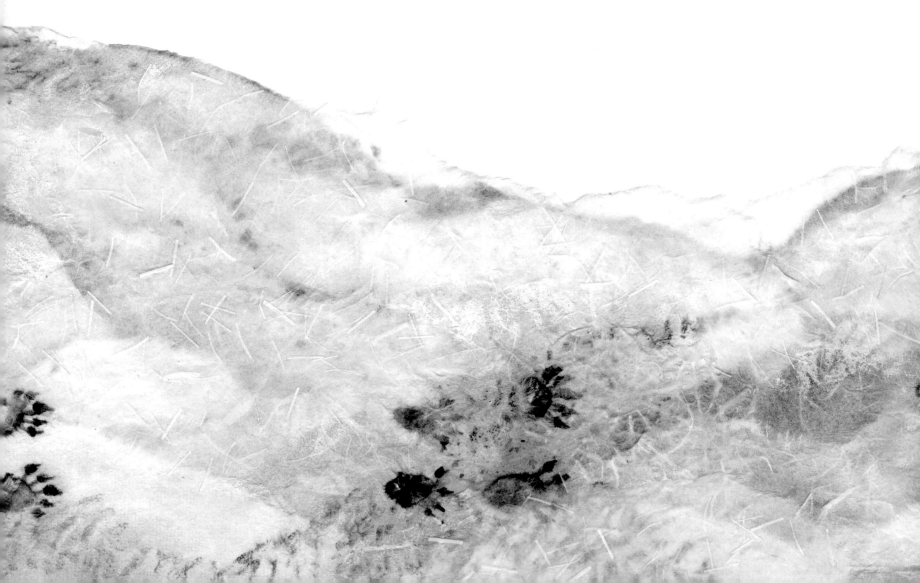

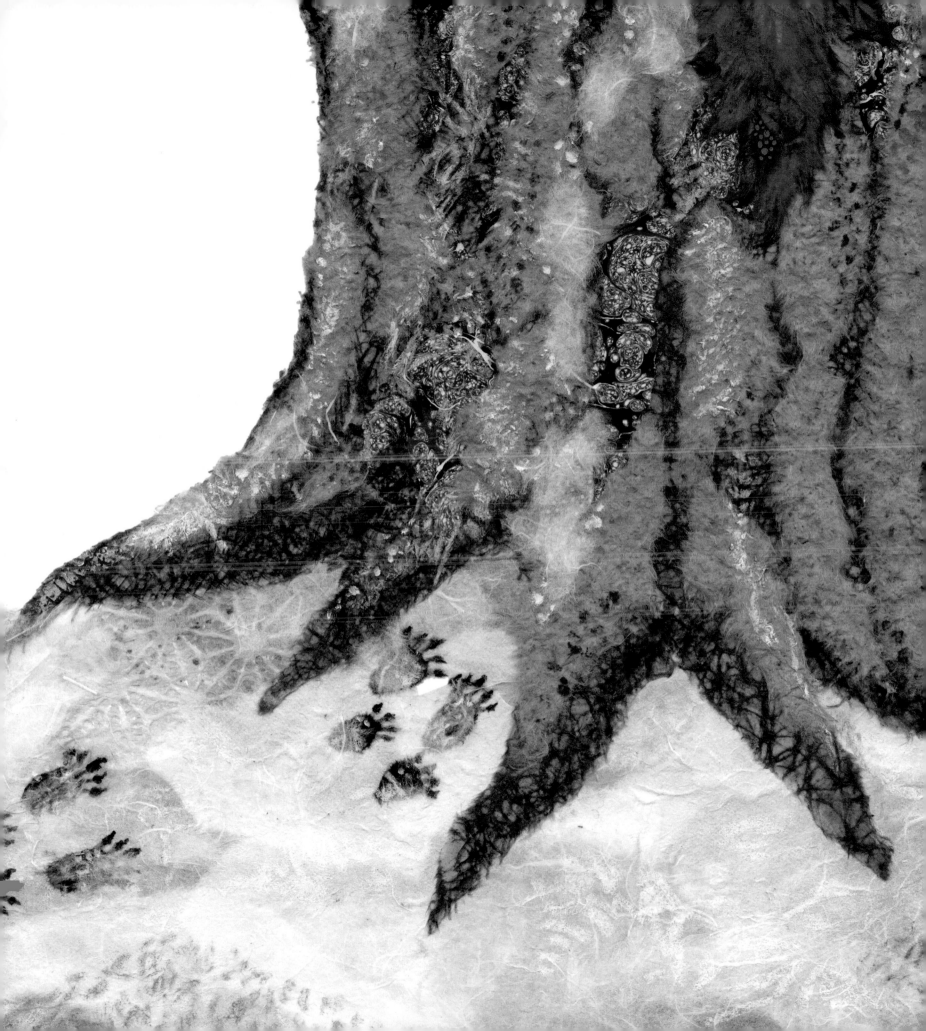

A hungry red squirrel!

Like hares, squirrels hop! They have four toes on their front feet and five toes on their back feet. They have a strong sense of smell that helps them find the seeds they bury before winter.

Look! Look! Tracks in the snow!
Tracks with lines,
Tracks like a kite.

A waddling wild duck!

Water birds have webbing between their toes
that gives their tracks a distinctive shape.
Ducks don't feel the cold in their feet because
blood runs through their body in a special way:
it lets their feet stay cold while their body remains
warm. They have waterproof feathers, which means
they can stay dry underwater!

Look! Look! Tracks in the snow!
Tracks like diamonds . . .
Where do they go?

Who left the tracks
in the fresh, deep snow?

A bushy-tailed fox!

Foxes' prints are similar to those of dogs and wolves. They have triangular heel pads and four toes. Foxes can lie outside covered in snow because they have a big bushy tail that they wrap around their body. A fox's hearing is so good that it can hear the squeak of a mouse at the far end of the wood!